MARKETING MASTERY

MAP: *Discover, Define, and Dominate Your Digital Space*

Badmus Owolabi

Table of Contents

Introduction

These days, launching your own business is everything. Sadly, a lot of recently established business owners mistakenly think that building a website is enough to make money; they need to do more to succeed. Even though every business needs a dedicated website, if that's all you do, you're not actually in business. Too many aspiring company entrepreneurs lack the patience and dedication necessary to thoroughly investigate a market to ascertain whether it would be profitable for them. The only way to lay a strong foundation for an internet business that succeeds is to identify a profitable niche and then develop content, goods, and services for that market. The best approach to achieving success is to choose a lucrative niche. Success and the kind of revenue that the majority of internet business proprietors require to justify their everyday endeavors. If you're enthused about all the amazing ideas you have for making money online, it can be very easy to end up not choosing a profitable topic. Additionally, it is simple to focus on a subject that you have heard is well-liked and where people are making enormous sums of money through online sales. When it comes to managing your own business, enthusiasm and passion are important, but doing your homework before jumping in headfirst is just as important. Before releasing new items to the public, all of the major corporations in the world take the time to thoroughly research the market. The study they carry out enables them to determine whether the general audience is interested in the possible offering. Regretfully, most inexperienced entrepreneurs make mistakes in this regard. Rather than conducting adequate research beforehand, they first invest time and money in developing a new product, then debut it and attempt to create a market for it, only to be confronted with disappointment and a product that no one wants to purchase.

The first step in running a successful internet business is identifying a paying customer base. When a paying market is identified, you can develop a product specifically for it and then introduce it by marketing to the identified paying market.

The most effective niche marketing plans and techniques are predicated on carrying out in-depth research and establishing trusting bonds with potential clients in your industry. Rather than conducting adequate research beforehand, they first invest time and money in developing a new product, then debut it and attempt to create a market for it, only to be confronted with disappointment and a product that no one wants to purchase.

The first step in running a successful internet business is identifying a paying customer base. When a paying market is identified, you can develop a product specifically for it and then introduce it by marketing to the identified paying market. The most effective niche marketing plans and techniques are predicated on carrying out in-depth research and establishing trusting bonds with potential clients in your industry.

There are many well-liked niches available, but not all of them will be lucrative. It will be far more profitable for you to produce goods for consumers who are prepared to pay a fair price for genuine solutions to the issues they are facing, even though you can still make some money from bargain hunters. This is the cornerstone of an internet business that will succeed and last. To achieve success in the online business world, you must locate satisfied and devoted clients who will make repeat purchases from you. You will even have some clients who are willing to purchase any new product you introduce if you follow all the correct procedures. But if you don't conduct the necessary research from the beginning, you may find that your business isn't feasible after investing hours of your time and effort into it. Until you are certain that you have selected a niche in a lucrative industry, your efforts to launch your blog or website and provide a product for sale will be in vain. The money you need to succeed and reach your financial objectives will start to come in once you've chosen the appropriate niche in a lucrative market.

Chapter 1- Defining the Essence of a Niche: What Is It Exactly?

The niche you choose at the outset of your business is one of the most crucial choices you will make if you want to operate a profitable blog or website. Anything you want to design, including its UX design and so on, will be impacted by this one choice. Before you've even switched on your computer, at this stage, you'll select your possible monetization alternatives. Although there is no such thing as a bad niche, some are considerably more profitable than others, and some are far more difficult to get into. What, though, is a niche?

What Exactly is a Niche?

A product group or area of interest is called a niche. Dog training is one fascinating specialty; an example of a product group niche would be electric lights. People look for things in these two categories on the Internet, and they look for things because they want to find solutions to their problems. They are searching for tangible solutions to their difficulties, or they are searching for information on the subject so they can handle the situation on their own. A niche market offers a means of providing solutions to issues in return for money. It's possible that those looking for dog training online are prepared to spend money on solutions to their canine's behavioral issues. Though it is much more likely that someone searching for electric lighting is looking to purchase lighting equipment, they may also be looking for information.

For an online business, a micro-niche is significantly more beneficial than a general niche. Solar garden lighting or husky dog training are two examples of micro-niches. People are looking for particular items in these situations; therefore, if you are creating a micro-niche website, you may more precisely target these potential clients. You may increase your chances of making a sale by showing products on your website that are precisely matched to what customers are looking for. Selecting a micro-niche also has the benefit of having millions of options. There are still lucrative micro-niches with minimal competition to be found today. This will allow you to enter a market that is experiencing difficulties and provide that market with a solution that they won't be able to find elsewhere. The ability to identify these niches is the key. Online business entrepreneurs can locate possibilities with minimal competition by focusing on niche markets, particularly micro-niche markets. Finding micro-niches where there is little competition yet a high volume of searches is the tricky part. These micro-niches are hard to identify, but once you do, they may be quite profitable. In case you are unable to generate revenue from these websites by offering physical or informational things, you may always employ pay-per-click advertising.

Knowing Niche Marketing

Marketing your goods or services to a certain subset of potential clients within a much wider clientele is known as niche marketing. This is carried out due to the fact that businesses that aim to serve a larger consumer base frequently fail to meet a requirement. Otherwise, there exists a need for a certain item that isn't being provided. A potential market is eager to pay you for what you can provide them if you can meet their desires. Consider internet marketing as an example. There are numerous sub-niches within the Internet marketing niche, such as Google Ads, PPC, articles, and search engine marketing. These sub-niches can be further narrowed down to encompass even more niche markets. You may, for instance, target the niche market of PPC advertisers who exclusively use Yahoo

Search Marketing or Google Ads. The demand for additional resources and information relevant to their enterprises has increased for these specific niche sectors. Those who only focus on the vast Internet marketing market are not the ones providing this information. Companies that concentrate mostly on those who use Google Ads won't be very interested in learning about article marketing, and individuals who are interested in PPC marketing won't be interested in article marketing. Because niche marketers directly address the issues that their target markets face, they are better able to serve the needs and requests of their niche clients. This is the reason why some businesses choose to market to specific niches.

The Oversaturation of Niche Markets

Due to the realisation by many entrepreneurs that Internet marketers and their products are oversaturating the market, niche marketing has grown to become one of the main methods of marketing over the years. Profiting from the huge Internet marketing market becomes considerably more difficult as a result. Because many experienced Internet marketers have extremely devoted clients who trust them and their products, it will be much harder for those who are new to the industry to break through. Because there is little to no competition in a certain niche, new internet marketers have a greater chance of competing in it or maybe dominating it. Your chances of succeeding and securing a lucrative share of a niche are higher the more narrowly focused you can be.

Fortunately, there's a lucrative niche to be found in almost every business. A significant number of prosperous online marketers achieve financial success by focusing on many niches, some of which are unrelated to one another. After conducting the required research to ascertain whether there is a lucrative niche market for a good or service they can provide, they choose a domain name, create a website, and begin marketing it to the target niche. Niche markets, however, don't always involve marketing. Any market, including those for dogs, gardening, home décor, literature, and more, can be divided into niches. Furthermore, based on the product, the target market, or both, any market can be divided into more manageable niches. With a seemingly limitless selection of niches available to you and new ones emerging daily, picking the best one for your company ought to be simple.

Chapter 2- Understanding the Significance of Discovering a Niche

Astute business owners carry out thorough market research with an emphasis on attempting to comprehend the consumer behaviour of the target audience that is interested in that niche in order to offer their goods and services to that specific group of customers. This specifically addresses their wants, needs, and worries.

You can begin catering to them as much as possible by offering them a variety of things for sale at different price points if your research indicates that customers are interested in the niche product or service that you intend to market. You must keep in mind that certain products in a certain category will appeal to a far wider audience than others. Customers seeking advanced golf information in the hopes of becoming professional players will be less interested in advanced golf items, for instance, than in beginner-oriented golf products. You can enhance volume sales by concentrating on beginner-friendly products, which will allow you to provide a cheaper price point to a larger number of people. Even though there might not be as many advanced students searching for golf-related material and products, the premium knowledge you can offer could fetch a far greater price than eBooks geared towards beginners.

If you are regarded as an authority in your field, you can charge a lot more for courses, coaching programmes, multimedia packages, membership programmes, and other comparable offerings that you might provide to advanced students. This is due to the fact that, within reason, you can charge more for the goods and services you provide in your sector, the more credentials you have. Finding the perfect niche involves more than just determining which one is the most profitable; it also involves determining what customers are truly willing to pay to have their problems answered, so you must set your price point appropriately. If you wish to enter the market with a $39 product and their average pricing is $29.95, you will need to provide a clear explanation for why your product is more valuable.

Your qualifications, experience, and the extras you can provide will surely help to allay a customer's concerns and persuade them that the additional expense is worthwhile. But the only way you can convince them to spend the additional amount is if you are aware of competing offers so that you may outbid them. You will find out if your topic is lucrative as you conduct studies on it and whether other users are prepared to pay top dollar for the kind of insider knowledge you can offer. When conducting research for your niche, you should also consider the client life cycle within the specialty. Even though they may begin as beginners, if they stay in the niche and keep learning, they will eventually need to acquire intermediate or advanced knowledge. You will be able to close deals with your consumers repeatedly if you have a thorough understanding of their life cycle. The basic rule of thumb in niche marketing is that 20% of your consumers will account for 80% of your profits. Taking good care of your clients increases the likelihood that they will stay loyal to your business. Additionally, they have a far higher chance of buying the new goods and services you provide them that will satisfy their requirements. By automating a process with a variety of offers preloaded on an email marketing platform, which can then be periodically distributed to your clients and prospects, you may begin to generate revenue around the clock.

All you need to do to maintain a successful product is keep directing people to your sales page.

Regarding requirements, cost points, and customer behaviour, each niche is unique. For this reason, before deciding which niche to market in, you should conduct a study. This will enable you to determine whether a niche is lucrative as well as viable before wasting your time, effort, or money. As you start your business, this might assist you in setting reasonable expectations and goals.

Chapter 3 - What Makes Choosing the Right Niche Profitable?

You must first ascertain whether there is a market for the product or service you are selling before you can begin designing it and before you waste too much time creating a website and content. This implies that you should consider how you will market your offering and whether the niche you are considering will work with your intended company plan. It is critical to realise that the profitability of certain niches varies greatly.

What makes a niche profitable?

You must think about your monetization alternatives in order to completely comprehend this. Public relations is one of these choices. This calls for adding Google advertisements or banner advertisements to your website. Because you are ultimately driving users away from your site each time they click on an advertisement, this is likely the least successful method of monetizing your specialty. Additionally, you should think about whether those marketers are prepared to pay for your traffic. They need to find a way to profit from your website visits more than you do. Most certainly, these advertisers are profiting from the sales of their products. In the event that they are making sales, they will be able to retain the majority of the revenue from each customer while also maintaining their brand's engagement. This is the ultimate goal you should have for your website. You can accomplish this by selling a product that you did not develop or produce your own product, preferably a digital product like an eBook. We call this kind of advertising affiliate marketing. You can, of course, also market services. Prior to selecting your topic, keep in mind that certain themes are better suited for products that you may sell considerably faster than others. This will ultimately affect your advertising budget. Your advertisers won't be willing to pay much to appear on your website if there is nothing in your niche that they can sell. What does this imply for the profitability of a niche, then? It implies that you will make the most money from niches with a large number of products that can be offered.

Some High-Earning Niches to Consider

Offering a type of investment for the customer is one of the most obvious reasons a specialty could be profitable. People would be happy to pay for information on a blog about investing, for instance, as they should be able to make more money from that knowledge than they would have to pay for it. The same holds true for business-related subjects. In principle, they would make their money back, so people spend thousands of dollars on online courses to learn how to monetize websites. Any niche that makes the promise to improve the customer's life in a quantifiable way is also likely to be profitable. This is the point at which you should think about your value proposition or the way you will improve people's lives. For this reason, fitness is an extremely profitable niche to be in. Spending a lot of money on exercise equipment or fitness books is common among those who think they will reap the benefits of toned abs and bulging biceps. They may then live longer, have greater self-assurance, and generally feel better as a result of this. Most individuals find this to be a really alluring opportunity, and they would gladly part with their hard-earned cash to pursue it.

The cost of the goods or services you are selling is something else to think about. Having more expensive things up for sale implies that you might be able to make more money from your website. You may become very wealthy as a writer if you write about sports automobiles. Travel blogs' attractiveness to travel agencies and websites like Expedia and Orbitz for advertising is another reason why they can be quite profitable. If your niche lacks high-ticket items, an alluring value offer, or the prospect of investment, it's simply not clearly viable and you will need to be a little more inventive. For instance, you may like to earn money by assisting clients in finding lodging so that you can get paid a commission. Perhaps your goal is to develop your website first, then expand into new regions. Before you begin the process of selecting your niche, be sure you've thought about all of this.

Chapter 4 - Choosing your Niche

You should start by writing down your thoughts for a niche you would like to work in and the reasons behind your interest as you embark on your online niche business. There are a variety of reasons why you would like to work in a specific specialisation. Because their chosen niche is in high demand and on the rise, many people choose it. That is acceptable if you plan to enter new and developing areas, but in order to stay ahead of the curve, you must be willing to work hard and be nimble. But although some trends move quickly, others aren't all that fascinating, intriguing, or even long-lasting. Prestigious occasions like the Olympics or the presidential election can create a lot of hype and desire for mementos, but as soon as the event is finished, the excitement fades rapidly. These kinds of You will only be able to stay in business for a certain amount of time in niche markets before you need to look for another successful specialty.

<u>Choosing an Everlasting Niche</u>

We refer to niches that endure over time as evergreen niches. These markets are considerably more sustainable and can maintain your company for many years, even though they might not generate the same buzz as the newest technology or event. Being evergreen refers to having goods and services that can continue to bring in money for you year after year. It's advisable to look for a niche that is both timeless and engaging enough for you to look forward to working in it on a daily basis.

<u>Choosing a Niche Based on Your Interests</u>
Many find it easy to select a specialty since they build their businesses on their own hobbies and areas of expertise. It can be advantageous to be an authority on what customers want to hear about in that market. Possessing in-depth knowledge and experience in the chosen area will also provide you with a fair indication of its potential profitability. Put another way, if you personally purchase things in the niche, there's a good probability that other people will do the same. But it's important to remember that individuals won't always act the way you expect them to. Even though you may

think your idea is fantastic, if you don't do enough research into the sector, it can fail, and you'll discover there is absolutely no market for it. You must pay attention to what people are saying in order to identify the issues and difficulties they are facing and then present a solution. You may find out what steps your potential clients are willing to take to accomplish their own goals by doing in-depth research and getting to know them better. It will save you months of laborious work with no return if you take the time to do a thorough analysis before you begin working on your product.

Selling as an Affiliate

When you first start your business, affiliate marketing is the simplest way to generate revenue. You may access millions of products that you are already aware are in demand by signing up as an associate for well-known companies like Amazon. You can start making commissions as high as 15 percent, depending on the compensation scheme you select and the products you are selling in particular niches. Numerous well-known businesses, such as Amazon and eBay, have internal affiliate programs of their own. Through a marketplace that manages the program on their behalf, other businesses run their affiliate programs.

Although producing your own goods and services to sell is the most profitable method to become successful in your industry, there are a few reasons you might want to consider launching an affiliate marketing business first. Above all, affiliate marketing is a means through which you can turn a profit as soon as you launch an internet business. It also requires less effort and time to get going. One strong indicator that the niche is profitable is the things you can offer through an affiliate program. When you are ready to create your own products or services, you may base your selection on the research you did as an affiliate marketer. Research can also assist you in identifying gaps in your current offerings of goods and services. Starting as an affiliate marketer is also a terrific way to learn a lot about marketing, which will help you later on when you start selling your own goods and services. Typically, a manager with experience in creating compelling offers, ideas, and visuals oversees affiliate marketing programs.

Frequently, they offer helpful pointers and advice to affiliate marketers that will be beneficial when they start selling their own goods in the future.

In conclusion, the more revenue streams your company can acquire, the more money it can make. Even though your monthly commission checks might not be large at first, how much more you can make depends on how many things you can market.

Chapter 5 - Initiating Your Niche Research Journey

Finding the keywords your target market uses is a crucial first step in determining the niche market you wish to pursue. You must ascertain the keywords that they are entering into search engines and apply those terms to look for subjects and goods associated with your industry. Your research will reveal the issues that the target market faces and the difficulties that need to be fixed. Understanding the keywords that are associated with your specialty will enable you to reach the greatest number of clients who are seeking goods and services that are directly relevant to your niche. Consequently, this can enable you to make a sizable profit in your specialty.

You have the opportunity to discover all the pertinent keywords that your target audience uses by using Google's Keyword Planner. You can begin identifying the keywords with the highest earning potential once you've determined which terms and phrases are related to your selected topic. Three methods exist for determining a keyword's potential for profit:

- *Minimal rivalry*
- *High volume of searches*
- *Low effort or cost to score highly*

Finding Hot Keywords

You may calculate the quantity of prospective visitor traffic for each keyword in your niche by using Google Ads' Keyword Planner. It displays the keywords that people are using together with any related keywords that may help you figure out what else your potential clients could need. Your study must be thorough and targeted if you want to select a profitable niche. Until you believe you have covered every term and phrase a potential customer might use to search for your good or service, you should test as many keywords as you can.

Whether or not there is a sufficient monthly number of potential clients actively searching for the good or service you are attempting to sell should be your first point of data analysis. Additionally, you should find out if other companies are already profitable from comparable goods or services. Search engines like Google and Bing, as well as Google's

Keyword Planning Tool, can be used to achieve this.

<u>How To Organize Your Keywords</u>

Sorting your terms and phrases into groups is the next step. You can achieve this by segmenting all of your keywords into collections of related terms and phrases. "Digital camera," for instance, is a keyword term that may be further broken down into "underwater digital camera," "underwater digital cameras," and "digital underwater camera." One group might contain these, while another group would contain "underwater digital camera cases," "digital camera cases," and so on. Your keywords should be divided into a group that receives at least 2,000 searches per month. Finding a common mindset across groups of people who are currently searching for comparable goods, services, details, advantages, or qualities is the rationale for this.

By focusing even more on the top ten keywords you've investigated, you can find even more potential customers for your goods or services. You want to attempt and locate at least 100,000 searches each month using these ten keywords. You can use the Google Keyword Planner Tool to find even more targeted long-tail keywords by adding each of your keywords to it. The next action is to begin scanning your list for terms that will generate revenue. These buyer keywords indicate that information will be paid for. Brand names, model numbers, colours, cheap, buy, for sale, supplier, seller, etc. are some examples of these keywords. Customers are more likely to be prepared to buy when their search is more focused.

How to Test Your Keywords Live

Testing your keywords live on the internet is the most effective technique to determine their potential earnings. One way to achieve this is by incorporating keyword-focused material into a page on your existing website, blog, or social media accounts. Next, you can test every piece of content to see how it performs on Google and how much traffic it generates. Using this technique, you may identify the keywords that will drive organic traffic to your website, the ones that turn that traffic into sales, and the keywords that have a higher search engine ranking.

A keyword's potential for profit increases with the amount of traffic it receives when it ranks lower on search engines.

Chapter 6 - Building Relationships Within Your Niche

Having selected a lucrative niche, it is now the right moment to consider developing relationships within that area. Finding the most popular websites, blogs, forums, and discussion boards related to your niche will be necessary for this. Spend some time reading through each of these resources to find discussions on subjects related to your selected niche. List the top five concerns that you find are being considered. This will provide you with an excellent starting point for content ideas for your blog, newsletter, and even a special report that you can offer for free in exchange for your potential client's email addresses. By sharing content frequently on your social media accounts, you can keep your followers informed about your company and make it much simpler for them to tell anyone they know who might be interested in your goods or services. Make it a habit to consistently request shares and retweets, and educate your target audience on the actions you want them to perform at the appropriate times.

Making money was probably one of your primary motivations for starting an internet business. If this is your sole driving force, though, there's a good chance it will come through. Online users are not required to be courteous, in contrast to those in physical stores. You won't even know that they left your site when they clicked off, and you won't see them again. You'll have a better chance of staying in touch with them on a regular basis and developing a relationship that will help you further develop your brand if you can sign them up for your newsletter or an online course.

According to recent research, consumers need to be exposed to a brand or company at least 17 times before they begin to recognise it and comprehend what it stands for. Regretfully, there is rarely a second opportunity for an internet firm to establish a great first impression.

Email Marketing

You will have a vital line of communication with those who have expressed interest in your specialty thanks to your email marketing initiatives. With email marketing campaigns, you may provide your target audience with enticing reasons to subscribe, such as newsletters and exclusive reports. You can add your target demographic to a fresh list made just for new consumers if they buy something. It can be difficult to keep them on a list once you've got them on it. For this reason, it's a good idea to offer an e-course with multiple lessons that are distributed via autoresponder if you want to maintain contact with your target audience. If someone unsubscribes from your list, try to find out why they did so rather than taking it personally. There are those who will take the trouble to explain their unsubscription. If you have insulted someone in any way, some will walk away and never return your calls. You simply never know when a customer may reach their tipping point.

Your Social Media Networks

Relationship building within your expertise can also be facilitated by your social media networks. Facebook followers have the ability to like, comment on, and share your content. This implies that anything you post is likewise visible to everyone in their network. This is an excellent chance for relationship-building and marketing that can generate free traffic and purchases for you.

Your Newsletter

You have the opportunity to regularly provide your customers with fresh, engaging material that is relevant to your specialty through your newsletter. You can promote new products and services, offer quizzes, examine frequently asked questions in FAQs, and much more. To help them with the issues you know they are facing, you can utilise all the knowledge you've gleaned from the forums and discussion boards you've visited. By doing this, you are establishing connections and establishing yourself as an authority in your field without using pushy sales techniques. You are presenting them with offers that a client in your specialty would find desirable. You have the option to send the offers by email individually, on a specific day, or integrated into your newsletter. It all comes down to giving your clients the information they need and establishing a rapport with them to demonstrate how you are able to satisfy their wants. It all comes down to remaining on topic and providing them with a selection of options that are relevant to your specialty.

Chapter 6 - Closing Thoughts

Selecting a lucrative specialty is the surest route to success for your internet venture. There will always be gaps in the market where people's needs for particular brands and series aren't being satisfied, which presents you with the chance to fill those voids. The unmet needs can be advantageous to a small firm like yours. The problem lies in figuring out which specialised market will best support the growth of your small business. You'll have less competition if your product is remarkable or unique.

It takes time, patience, effort, the correct tools, and the capacity to formulate good questions and comprehend the responses you get to investigate a niche and decide if it is profitable.

Research is necessary if you want to succeed. You will only be wasting your time, money, and efforts if you decide not to conduct an in-depth study on your possible niche markets. It won't be easy to find the ideal niche for your company, but it will take some time. The rewards will come in the form of growing sales and increased revenue.